Copyright 2020 by Kenneth Reyes -All rights reserved.

No part of this publication may be reproduced, distributed, or transmitted in any form or by any means, including photocopying, recording, or other electronic or mechanical methods, without the prior written permission of the publisher, except in the case of brief quotations embodied in reviews and certain other non-commercial uses permitted by copyright law.

This Book is provided with the sole purpose of providing relevant information on a specific topic for which every reasonable effort has been made to ensure that it is both accurate and reasonable. Nevertheless, by purchasing this Book you consent to the fact that the author, as well as the publisher, are in no way experts on the topics contained herein, regardless of any claims as such that may be made within. It is recommended that you always consult a professional prior to undertaking any of the advice or techniques discussed within.This is a legally binding declaration that is considered both valid and fair by both the Committee of Publishers Association and the American Bar Association and should be considered as legally binding within the United States.

CONTENTS

Introduction 4
Breads 5
    Whole Wheat Bread 5
    White Bread 6
    French Bread 7
    Breakfast Biscuits 8
Breakfast Sandwiches 9
    French Toast Sandwich 9
    Sausage, Egg and Cheese Breakfast Biscuit 10
    Vegetable Breakfast Sandwich 11
    Breakfast Twisty Braid 12
    Egg and Avocado Sandwich 13
    Bagel and Lox 14
American Sandwiches 15
    Soft Shell Crab Po'boys 15
    Shrimp Po' Boys 16
    Philly Steak Sandwich 17
    Sloppy Joes 18
    Grilled Cheese Sandwich with Peppers 19
    Tangy Chicken Wraps 20
    Chicago-Style Hot Dog 21
    Slow-Cooker Brisket Sandwiches 22
    Pork Schnitzel Sandwiches 23
    Curried Tuna Salad Sandwich 24
    Monte Cristo Sandwich 25
    BBQ Pork Sandwiches 26
    Fried Haddock Sandwich 27
    Hot Pastrami Sandwich 28
    Open-Face Tuna Melt 29
    Reuben Sandwich 30
    Grilled Spicy Turkey and Bacon Sandwich 31
    Thanksgiving Leftovers Sandwich 32
Mediterranean Sandwiches 33
    Tuna Salad in Pita Pockets 33
    Grilled Vegetable Sandwich 34
    Greek-Style Chicken Salad Sandwich 35
    Falafel and Cucumber Sauce 36
    Chicken Souvlaki 37
    Hummus, Avocado Sandwich with Feta 38
    Hummus and Caramelized Onion Sandwich 39
    Croque Monsieur 40
    Paneer Sandwich 41
    Vietnamese Banh Mi 42

Thai Peanut Chicken Sandwich 43
Thai Beef Lettuce Wraps 44
Cuban Sandwich 45
Cucumber Tea Sandwiches 46
English Sausage Rolls 47
Herring and Onion on Pumpernickel 48
Chicken Parmesan Sandwich 49
Meatball Submarine 50
Russian Kielbasa Sandwich 51
Stromboli 52
Bean Burritos 53
Steak Torta 54

Introduction

What's so great about a sandwich? There are so many ways of preparing one, you could have a different dining experience every day and still want more.

Chances are, you started eating sandwiches when Mom prepared them for your lunch box. Are you still eating those same old sandwiches? This Sandwich Cookbook will introduce you to a huge variety of different flavors and ways of preparing sandwiches from around the world. And your kids will be able to enjoy something different than the usual tuna and PBJ.

Sandwiches are quick and handy for a tasty and nutritious breakfast, as well. Put together your favorite meats, vegetables and cheeses on a homemade biscuit that is so delicious, you'll never stop by that fast-food place again.

Sandwiches are still the perfect go-to for lunch – easy to prepare and pack. And with the recipes in this Sandwich Cookbook, you'll be dining in style. Whether it's a new take on old favorites, such as curried tuna or a spicy grilled cheese, or sandwiches that are new, vibrant and incredibly tasty, this Cookbook is filled with ideas.

Sandwiches are a favorite around the world, and you'll surprise your family with sandwich creations not only from America, but Europe and Asia, as well. A rich and creamy Croque Monsieur from Paris, a scrumptious beef wrap from Thailand or an exotic Banh Mi from Vietnam are at your fingertips with this Sandwich Cookbook. If you're in the mood for something simpler, we'll tell you how to prepare a Chicago-style hot dog to perfection.

If you love sandwiches, this Sandwich Cookbook will open up a whole new and fascinating world.

Breads

For the perfect sandwich, you need the best bread. Here, you'll find a few bread recipes that are far tastier than anything at the supermarket. It's easier to bake that incredible loaf of bread than you may imagine. And just imagine your kitchen filling with the intoxicating aroma of freshly baked bread....

Whole Wheat Bread

Whole wheat bread that gets some sweetness from added honey. It's very simple to prepare and punching the dough is quite the stress-reliever.

Cooking Time: 30 minutes
Servings: 3 loaves
Ingredients
- .50 oz. dry yeast
- ½ cup honey
- 5 cups white flour
- 1 cup oats
- 1 tbsp. sesame seeds (optional)
- 1 tsp. salt
- 2 cups whole wheat flour or as much as needed
- 2 tbsp. melted butter

Directions:
1. Stir ¼ cup honey and yeast into 3 ¼ cups of warm water.
2. Add the flour, oats, sesame seeds and thoroughly combine.
3. Set aside for 30 minutes.
4. Add another ¼ cup honey, melted butter and salt.
5. Stir 2 cups whole wheat flour into the mixture and combine
6. Lightly flour a surface.
7. Place the dough on the surface and knead until the dough loses some of its stickiness. Add additional whole wheat flour if necessary.
8. Transfer the dough into a lightly greased bowl.
9. Cover with a moist towel and let the dough double in size.
10. Really punch down on the dough.
11. Lightly butter 3 9 x 5 loaf pans.
12. Distribute the dough to the 2 pans.
13. Bake for 30 minutes at 350 degrees.
14. Remove from oven and brush with the additional melted butter.

White Bread

A wonderful bread with a soft middle and great crust. Perfect for so many sandwiches.

Cooking Times: 30 minutes
Servings: 2 loaves
Ingredients:
- .50 oz. dry yeast
- 3 tbsp. sugar
- 3 tbsp. Crisco
- 1 tbsp. salt
- 6 1/2 cups bread flour
- 2 tbsp. wheat gluten
- 1 tsp. olive oil
- 1 tbsp. melted butter

Directions:
1. Stir the yeast and sugar into 2 ½ cups of warm water.
2. Add the Crisco and salt.
3. Mix the flour and wheat gluten together.
4. Slowly, using only 1/4 cup each time, stir the flour into the Crisco mixture.
5. Thoroughly stir every time you add more flour.
6. Lightly flour a surface and transfer the dough.
7. Knead the dough gently for 8 minutes.
8. Grease a bowl with the olive oil and place the dough in the bowl. Coat with the oil.
9. Cover with a damp towel and let sit until the dough has doubled, 1 hour.
10. Punch the dough and return it to the floured surface.
11. Form 2 loaves.
12. Grease two loaf pans and fill each with 1 loaf.
13. Cover with a damp towel and let sit for 45 minutes.
14. Preheat the oven to 425 degrees.
15. Reduce the heat to 375 degrees and bake both loaves for 30 minutes.
16. Brush the top of both loaves with the melted butter.

French Bread

A great crusty French baguette. Note that in the final step before baking, you can add things like garlic, grated cheese or cinnamon to create garlic bread, cheesy bread or a cinnamon bread. loaf.

Cooking Time: 35 minutes
Servings: 2 loaves
Ingredients:
- .50 oz. dry yeast
- 6 cups bread flour
- 1 tbsp. salt
- 1 tablespoon white sugar
- 5 tbsp. softened butter
- 1 beaten egg white

Directions:
1. In a medium or large bowl, dissolve the yeast in half a cup of warm water. Let sit for 10-15 minutes.
2. Add 2 more cups of water, half the flour, sugar, salt and the butter.
3. Stir the Ingredients thoroughly.
4. Let the dough sit for 10 minutes.
5. Repeat this four more times – stir and let sit.
6. Place the dough onto a floured surface and knead for just a few minutes.
7. If you want to be creative, this is the time to cover your hands with garlic, grated cheese or cinnamon and lightly knead it into the bread to create a specialty loaf.
8. Cut the dough in half and create two 9 x 12 loaves.
9. Place the loaves on a greased baking sheet.
10. Cut 3 or 4 slashes into the top of each loaf and brush with the egg white.
11. Cover with a damp towel for 30 minutes.
12. Bake for 35 minutes.

Breakfast Biscuits

We know you've been sneaking into those fast food chains for their breakfast biscuits. Now, you can bake delicious biscuits at home and created a variety of incredible breakfast sandwiches. They're great with dinner, too. Yummy.

Cooking Time: 15 minutes
Servings: 10

- 2 cups white flour
- 2 tsp. baking powder
- ½ tsp. baking soda
- 1 tsp. salt
- 1 tbsp. white sugar
- 1/3 cup very cold butter
- 1 cup buttermilk

Directions:
1. Place all dry Ingredients in a food processor.
2. Pulse to combine.
3. Add the butter, making sure it is ICE COLD.
4. Keep pulsing until the butter is crumbled into pea-sized pieces.
5. Add the buttermilk and combine into a dough.
6. Remove the dough and roll into a long cylinder the width of a coffee cup.
7. Wrap the dough in plastic and refrigerate for at least 2 hours.
8. Preheat the oven to 425.
9. Cut the chilled dough into 1-inch pieces.
10. Place the biscuits on a greased baking sheet.
11. Bake for 15 minutes.

Breakfast Sandwiches
French Toast Sandwich

You like French toast? You like bacon? Have we got a sandwich for you!!

Cooking Time: 16 minutes
Servings: 2
Ingredients:
- 2 beaten eggs
- ¼ cup milk
- ½ tsp. cinnamon
- Dash of nutmeg
- 2 tbsp. butter
- 4 slices white or sourdough bread
- 4 slices bacon
- 2 eggs
- 4 tbsp. maple syrup

Directions:
1. Combine the eggs, milk, cinnamon and nutmeg in a bowl.
2. Coat each bread slice with the mixture.
3. Heat the butter in the skillet.
4. Fry each slice under they are golden brown. Set aside.
5. Fry the bacon in a skillet. Set aside
6. Fry the eggs (in some of the bacon fat is fine).
7. Lay out two of the French toast slices
8. Top with 2 bacon strips and 1 egg.
9. Drizzle some maple syrup over each toast slice.
10. Top the toast slices with the remaining 2 slices to create a sandwich.

Sausage, Egg and Cheese Breakfast Biscuit

Use the biscuit recipe in this book for an eye-opening breakfast. Much better than the ones you get at the fast food places.

Cooking Time: 20 minutes
Servings: 6
Ingredients:
- 6 homemade biscuits or store-bought frozen biscuits
- ¾ lb. breakfast pork sausage
- 6 eggs
- 4 tbsp. milk
- Salt and pepper to taste
- 4 tbsp. butter
- 6 Swiss or cheddar cheese slices

Directions:
1. Heat a skillet.
2. Create 6 pork sausage patties and fry 4 minutes each side, or until done.
3. Clean the skillet and melt the butter
4. Whisk together the eggs and milk and season with salt and pepper.
5. Scramble the eggs until done, about 5 minutes.
6. Slice the biscuits in half.
7. Top half the slices with cheese.
8. Place the biscuits on a baking sheet.
9. Brown at 375 degrees for 7 minutes – cheese should be melted and biscuits should be brown.
10. Top those biscuits halves with cheese with the scrambled eggs and sausage patties.
11. Create sandwiches by placing the remaining biscuit halves on top.

Vegetable Breakfast Sandwich

Sometimes, you just want something healthy for breakfast. This sandwich will provide you with the substance to make it to lunch.

Cooking Time: 4 minutes
Servings: 2
Ingredients:
- 2 whole grain English muffins
- 3 egg whites
- 1 cup chopped spinach
- 4 tomato slices
- 1 sliced avocado
- Salt and pepper to taste

Directions:
1. Split and toast the English muffins
2. While the muffins are toasting, whisk the eggs whites to a peak.
3. Scramble the egg whites in skillet for 4 minutes.
4. Lay out 2 toasted muffin halves
5. Top each with half the scrambled egg whites, 2 tomato slices, 2 avocado slices and half the chopped spinach.
6. Season with salt and pepper.
7. Top with the remaining 2 muffin halves to create a sandwich.

Breakfast Twisty Braid

These make a fun and easy family breakfast. Using store-bought rolls makes this easy to assemble.

Cooking Time: 30 minutes
Servings: 6
Ingredients:
- ½ cup milk
- 4 oz. softened cream cheese
- 1 tsp. chopped chives
- 8 eggs
- Salt and pepper to taste
- 2 packages crescent roll dough
- ½ cup crumbled cooked breakfast sausage
- 1 cup shredded Cheddar cheese

Directions:
1. Preheat oven to 375 degrees.
2. Brown the sausage meat in a skillet for 2-3 minutes.
3. Add the chopped onions and stir for another 2 minutes.
4. Set aside
5. Use a hand beater to whisk the cream cheese, chives and milk.
6. Add the eggs, salt and pepper and beat for another minute.
7. Lightly grease a baking sheet.
8. Arrange 1 package of frozen crescent rolls to create a rectangle.
9. Arrange the second package so the long sides overlap and the short part of the triangle hang over the baking sheet.
10. Place the sausage and onions in the center of the crescent dough.
11. Add the eggs over the meat and top with the shredded cheese.
12. Take the corners of the dough that are over the baking sheet and create a braid.
13. Bake for 30 minutes.
14. Cut into slices and serve.

Egg and Avocado Sandwich

Not only is this sandwich super-delicious, avocado is one of the healthiest foods. Can't beat that combination. If you want, you can reduce the cheese slices to two.

Cooking Time: 12 minutes
Servings: 2
Ingredients:
- 2 tbsp. butter
- 4 slices white or wheat bread
- Salt and pepper to taste
- 1 small sliced tomato
- 4 Swiss cheese or cheddar cheese slices
- 1 small sliced avocado
- 4 eggs

Directions:
1. Top the bread slices with cheese and toast in the oven for 7 minutes at 350 degrees.
2. Melt 2 tbsp. butter in a skillet.
3. Fry the eggs and crack the yolks.
4. Top 2 of the bread slices with the fried eggs.
5. Add the sliced tomatoes and sliced avocado.
6. Season with salt and pepper.
7. Top each slice with the remaining 2 toasted bread slices.

Bagel and Lox

This breakfast is sheer heaven. If you can't find lox, use smoked salmon, but the saltier lox adds some pizzazz. Any bagel is fine, but you don't want to overpower the delicate lox or salmon, so unless you're set on a bagel-with-everything, a plain bagel may work best.

Cooking Time: 0
Servings: 1
Ingredients:
- 1 sliced bagel
- 4 thin slices of lox
- 1 large red onion slice
- 1 large tomato slice
- ½ tsp capers
- Dash of lemon juice.

Directions:
1. Lightly toast the bagel in the toaster or oven.
2. Top – in this order – with lox, tomato slice, onion and capers.
3. Spritz with a dash of lemon juice.

American Sandwiches
Soft Shell Crab Po'boys

These are a Louisiana favorite. The cornmeal helps give them a nice crunch.

Ingredients:
- 8 soft shell crabs
- ½ cup flour
- ½ cup corn meal
- 2 beaten eggs
- 2 tbsp. Old Bay Seasoning
- Salt and pepper to taste
- ¼ cup canola oil
- 8 sliced French baguettes
- 3 cups cabbage slaw
- 2 sliced tomatoes
- 1 cup tartar sauce

Directions:
1. Clean and rinse the crabs
2. Lay out three shallow bowls and fill them with the flour, cornmeal and beaten eggs.
3. Season with crabs with Old Bay Seasoning, salt and pepper.
4. Dredge the crabs through the flour, eggs, then the cornmeal.
5. Bring the canola oil to a high temperature in a large skillet.
6. When the oil is hot enough, place the crabs in the skillet and fry for 3 minutes each side.
7. Place the fried crabs in the sliced baguettes
8. Top with the slaw and 2 tomato slices
9. Serve with tartar sauce

Shrimp Po' Boys

The secret to these heavenly shrimp po'boys is the remoulade sauce. Be sure to make enough. You can use frozen shrimp, but the fresher the shrimp, the better the po'boy.

Cooking Time: 15 minutes
Servings: 4
Ingredients:

- ½ cup canola oil
- 4 French baguettes
- 1 tsp. garlic
- 2 tbsp. soften butter
- 3 beaten eggs
- 2 tbsp. Cajun seasoning
- ¾ white flour
- 1 lb. peeled and deveined raw shrimp
- 2 cups bread crumbs
- 2 cups shredded Napa cabbage

Ingredients for Remoulade Sauce

- 1/2 cup mayonnaise
- 2 tbsp. hot mustard
- 1 tablespoon horseradish
- 1 tbsp. Old Bay Seasoning
- 1 tsp. pickle juice
- 1 tsp. minced garlic
- ½ tsp. paprika
- Dash of hot sauce (optional)

Directions:
1. Mix together the minced garlic and the butter.
2. Spread the mixture on the sliced baguettes.
3. Place the baguettes on a baking sheet and toast for 6-7 minutes.
4. Heat the canola oil in a skillet.
5. Lay out three shallow dishes.
6. Stir together the flour and Cajun seasoning and place in 1 dish.
7. Place the beaten egg on another dish and the bread crumbs in the third.
8. Dredge the shrimp through the flour, the eggs, then the breadcrumbs.
9. When the oil is hot, fry the shrimp until they are nice and brown. If needed, do this in batches.
10. Drain the shrimp on paper towels.
11. Spoon the remoulade sauce onto the toasted baguettes.
12. Fill each baguette with fried shrimp and diced Napa cabbage.
13. To create the remoulade sauce, combine all Ingredients in a bowl.
14. Serve the remoulade sauce with the sandwiches.

Philly Steak Sandwich

A wonderful sandwich from Philadelphia. Be sure to brown the onions until they are sweet and caramelized. This recipe has a combination of 3 shredded cheeses for some maximum flavor. If you don't have all 3, you can use either the mozzarella or the Monterey Jack, but combining them is optimal. And make sure the steak is sliced very thin.

Cooking Time: 30 minutes
Servings: 4
Ingredients:
- 1 cup mayonnaise
- 3 minced garlic cloves
- 2 tbsp. olive oil
- 1 lb. sirloin steak strips
- 2 sliced onions
- 1 chopped red bell pepper
- 1 chopped green bell pepper
- 1 cup sliced mushrooms
- Salt and pepper to taste
- 4 hoagie rolls
- 1 cup combination shredded Parmesan, Monterey Jack and Mozzarella

Directions:
1. Stir the minced garlic into the mayonnaise and refrigerate.
2. Preheat the oven to 500 degrees.
3. Heat the olive oil in a skillet.
4. Caramelized the onions on medium heat until they are browned, about 15 minutes.
5. Add the beef slices, pepper slices, mushrooms, salt and pepper.
6. Continue frying until the beef is browned and the peppers tender.
7. Transfer the beef/vegetable mix to a plate.
8. Line up the hoagies and spread the inside with the chilled mayonnaise mixture.
9. Fill each hoagie with the beef/pepper mixture.
10. Add the shredded cheeses on top.
11. Place the hoagies under the broiler until the cheese starts to bubble – about 4 minutes.

Sloppy Joes

These sandwiches are called sloppy for a good reason. Have a huge stack of napkins on hand and enjoy.

Cooking Time: 45 minutes
Servings: 6
Ingredients:
- 1 lb. ground beef
- 4 tbsp. chopped onion
- ½ tsp. garlic powder
- Salt and pepper to taste
- ½ cup ketchup
- ¼ cup BBQ sauce
- ½ tsp. yellow mustard
- 3 tsp. brown sugar
- 1 tsp. white sugar
- 2 tsp. white vinegar
- 1 tsp Worcestershire sauce

Directions:
1. Brown the beef and onions in a skillet.
2. Drain off the fat.
3. Add the remaining Ingredients and stir thoroughly.
4. Cover the skillet and simmer for 35-40 minutes
5. Serve on hamburger buns.

Grilled Cheese Sandwich with Peppers

It's time to rethink your grilled cheese sandwich. This is grilled cheese grown-up-style, with chopped peppers. You'll love the added kick.

Cooking Time: 8 minutes
Servings: 2
Ingredients:
- 2 tbsp. butter
- 4 slices white bread
- ¼ tsp. garlic powder
- 2 slices American cheese
- 2 slices Swiss cheese
- ½ sliced tomato
- 2 tbsp. chopped onions
- 1 chopped jalapeno pepper or ½ chopped serrano pepper

Directions:
1. Melt the butter in a skillet.
2. Place two slices of bread in the skillet.
3. Dust with garlic powder.
4. To each slice, add 1 slice of both cheeses, tomato, onions and the chopped peppers.
5. Top with the remaining bread slices and fry for 4 minutes.
6. Turn the sandwich over and fry for another 4 minutes, adding more butter if necessary.

Tangy Chicken Wraps

A tangy, spicy/sweet sandwich that's an easy lunch. The filling is also delicious with rice. Or you can add rice to the filling. So many options …

Cooking Time: 20 minutes
Servings: 8
Ingredients:
- ½ cup plain Greek yogurt
- ¼ cup diced cucumbers
- 2 tbsp. honey
- ½ tsp. crushed red peppers
- Salt and pepper to taste
- 3 tbsp. olive oil
- 2 lb. chicken thinly sliced
- 1 cup diced tomatoes
- 2 tbsp. chopped chili pepper
- 8 flour tortillas

Directions:
1. In a bowl, stir the yogurt, cucumbers, pepper, crushed red peppers and 1 tbsp. honey.
2. Refrigerate for an hour.
3. Heat the oil in a skillet.
4. Sauté the chicken strips for 8 minutes.
5. Add the diced tomatoes, chopped chili pepper and remaining 1 tbsp. honey.
6. Simmer for 6-7 minutes.
7. Heat the tortilla in the oven for 4 minutes.
8. Top each tortilla with the yogurt mixture.
9. Spoon the tangy chicken mixture along the center and roll up the tortilla.
10. Fold the ends to close the sandwich.

Chicago-Style Hot Dog

It's a known fact that two things will get you run out of the City of Chicago – rooting against the Cubs and putting ketchup on your hot dog. The Chicago hot dog is as vibrant as the city itself, and it must be all-beef and the bun must be steamed.

Cooking Time: 8 minutes
Servings: 2
Ingredients:
- 2 all-beef hot dogs
- 2 hot dog buns
- 2 tbsp. mustard
- 2 tbsp. diced onions
- 2 tbsp. sweet relish
- 1 tomato, cut into wedges
- 2 dill pickle spears
- 4 pepperoncini peppers
- 1 tsp. celery salt

Directions:
1. Either boil or grill the hot dogs and set aside.
2. Boil a pot of water and insert a steamer basket.
3. Steam the buns for 3 minutes.
4. Insert the cooked hot dogs into the steamed buns.
5. The Ingredients should be added in the proper order: first the mustard, then the relish.
6. Add the chopped onions, 2 tomato wedges per bun and 2 pepperoncini peppers per bun.
7. Place the pickle spear along the side of the bun.
8. Sprinkle with celery salt.
9. Hide the ketchup and enjoy.

Slow-Cooker Brisket Sandwiches

Slow cooking in a savory liquid makes a very tender brisket. Terrific for sandwiches.
Cooking Time: 6 hours
Servings: 6
Ingredients:
- 2 tbsp. canola oil
- 2-3 lb. brisket
- 1 cup cola
- ½ cup beef broth
- Salt and pepper
- 3 minced garlic cloves
- 1 tbsp. Worcestershire sauce
- 3 tbsp. tomato paste
- 2 tbsp. red wine vinegar
- 3 tbsp. Dijon mustard
- 1 bay leaf
- 2 large rolls

Directions:
1. Salt and pepper the brisket well.
2. Heat the oil in a skillet and brown the brisket for 10 minutes.
3. Place the brisket in a slow cooker.
4. Combine the remaining Ingredients, except the rolls, in a bowl and pour over the brisket
5. Cook on low for 6 hours and remove the bay leaf.
6. When the brisket has cooled, slice thinly and serve on toasted rolls.
7. Drizzle with some of the cooking liquid.

Pork Schnitzel Sandwiches

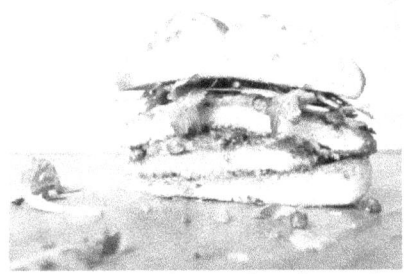

A crispy pork sandwich with cheese. It's easy to prepare and makes a great lunch.

Cooking Time: 10 minutes
Servings: 8
Ingredients:
- 8 small pork cutlets
- Salt and pepper to taste
- 1 cup white flour
- 1 tsp. sage
- 2 eggs
- 1/3 cup whole milk
- 1 ½ Panko breadcrumbs
- 3 tbsp. olive oil
- 4 tbsp. Dijon mustard
- 8 slices Swiss cheese
- 2 tbsp. butter
- 8 large rolls

Directions:
1. Season the pork cutlets with salt and pepper
2. Lay out 3 shallow dishes.
3. Beat the eggs and milk in 1 dish.
4. Place the flour and sage in a second dish and the breadcrumbs in a third dish.
5. Dredge each cutlet through the flour, the eggs and the breadcrumbs.
6. Heat the oil in a skillet and fry the pork cutlets for 5 minutes.
7. Flip the schnitzel and add a slice of cheese.
8. Fry for another 5 minutes, or until done.
9. Cut open the rolls and smear with some mustard
10. Add a pork schnitzel to each roll.
11. If desired, serve with onions and tomatoes.

Curried Tuna Salad Sandwich

This isn't the tuna sandwich your mom packed for lunch. The savory curry and the sweet raisins give this an exotic taste.

Cooking Time: 0
Servings: 1
Ingredients:
- 5 oz. can tuna packed in oil, drained
- 1 tbsp. mayonnaise
- 1 tbsp. sour cream
- 2 tbsp. raisins
- 1 chopped celery stalk
- 1 ½ tsp. curry powder
- Dash of salt
- Dash of garlic powder
- 4 tbsp. chopped scallions
- Chopped walnuts – optional
- 2 rye or white bread slices

Directions:
1. Thorough combine all the salad Ingredients.
2. Spread the tuna salad on a slice of bread and cover with the other slice.
3. Toasting the bread is optional but a good idea.

Monte Cristo Sandwich

This fried sandwich is a total indulgence, especially when dipped in syrup.
Cooking Time: 20 minutes
Servings: 6
Ingredients:
- 12 bread slices
- ¼ cup mayonnaise
- 2 tbsp. mustard
- 12 slices black forest ham
- 12 slices cooked turkey meat
- 6 slices Swiss cheese
- 1 egg
- 1 tsp baking powder
- ¼ tsp. salt
- 3 tbsp. milk
- ¼ cup water
- 1 ½ cup white flour
- 1 tbsp. maple syrup
- 4 tbsp. butter or more as needed

Directions:
1. Lay out 6 sandwich slices and spread them with the mustard and mayonnaise.
2. Top with turkey, Swiss cheese slices and ham slices.
3. Top with the remaining bread to create sandwiches
4. Whisk the eggs, water and milk in a shallow bowl.
5. Stir in the flour, baking powder, maple syrup and salt to create the batter.
6. Coat both sides of each sandwich thoroughly.
7. Melt the butter in a skillet.
8. Fry each sandwich 3-4 minutes both side.
9. Serve with extra maple syrup for dipping.

BBQ Pork Sandwiches

This BBP couldn't be easier to prepare, and it's so good. The beer really adds some extra flavor.

Cooking Time: 5 hours
Servings: 8
Ingredients:
- 1 cup beef broth
- 1 cup beer
- 3-4 lb. pork butt
- 18 oz. favorite BBQ sauce
- 8 baguettes or hamburger buns

Directions:
1. Pour the broth and beer into the slow cooker.
2. Add the pork butt.
3. Cook for 4 ½ hours on high.
4. Remove the pork and shred with a fork.
5. Place the shredded meat in a Dutch oven and combine with the BBQ sauce.
6. Roast at 350 degrees for 30 minutes,
7. Serve on baguettes or hamburger buns.

Fried Haddock Sandwich

A fabulous sandwich. Serve it with tartar sauce or the Remoulade sauce in this cookbook.

Cooking Time: 10 minutes
Servings: 4
Ingredients:
- ¼ canola oil
- 2 lbs. haddock or any firm white fish sliced into thick fillets
- 1/8 tsp. each salt, pepper, garlic salt and paprika
- 1 cup white flour
- 4 beaten eggs
- 1 cup Panko breadcrumbs
- 4 sandwich buns
- 4 tomato slices
- A few lettuces
- Onion slices (optional)

Directions:
1. Mix all the seasoning together in a bowl.
2. Coat the fish with the seasoning.
3. Heat the oil in a skillet.
4. Fill one shallow bowl with flour, a second with beaten eggs, a third with Panko breadcrumbs.
5. Dredge each fish fillet through the flour first, then the egg, and thirdly the breadcrumbs.
6. Fry the fish 5 minutes (depending on how thick) each side.
7. Drain the fish on paper towels.
8. Top the buns with the tomatoes, lettuce and onions and add a fish fillet to each.
9. Serve the sauce on the side or spread it on the bun.

Hot Pastrami Sandwich

A hot pastrami sandwich is a New York City standard. You want to place it in the oven at the end to really let the cheeses melt. And don't forget the pickles!

Cooking Time: 15 minutes
Servings: 4
Ingredients:
- 2 lbs. pastrami meat
- 1 cup beef broth
- 4 slice provolone cheese
- 4 slices Swiss cheese
- 8 sliced of rye bread
- 2 tbsp. sharp mustard
- Dill pickles

Directions:
1. Heat the beef broth in a pan and add the sliced pastrami.
2. Simmer for 5 minutes.
3. Divide the hot pastrami among 4 slices of rye.
4. Top with 1 slice of provolone and 1 slice of Swiss cheese.
5. Spread the remaining rye with the mustard and place on top of the other slices to create a sandwich.
6. Wrap each sandwich in aluminum foil.
7. Place the sandwich on a baking sheet.
8. Bake at 350 degrees for 10 minutes.
9. Serve with dill pickles.

Open-Face Tuna Melt

The trick to making these tasty tuna melts is to toast the bread before adding the salad. They are just perfect. Also, use firm tomatoes to prevent them from getting soggy.

Cooking Time: 10 minutes
Servings: 2
Ingredients:
- 4 sourdough bread slices
- 10 oz. albacore tuna
- 1/4 cup mayonnaise
- 4 tbsp. chopped celery
- ½ tsp. lemon juice
- Salt to taste
- 1 sliced tomato
- 8 slices of Gruyere cheese

Directions:
1. Preheat the oven to 375 degrees.
2. Place the bread in the oven to toast for 5 minutes.
3. While the bread is browning, combine all Ingredients except the tomatoes and cheese.
4. Remove the bread from the oven and lay on a flat surface
5. Cover each slice with tuna salad, 1 cheese slice, 1 tomato slice and another slice of cheese.
6. Place the bread slices on a baking sheet and return to the oven.
7. Cook for 5 minutes. The cheese should be melted.

Reuben Sandwich

The combination of Ingredients is what makes the essential Reuben. Don't deviate by using a different type of bread or meat. It's a total taste sensation. Weighing down the sandwich as it grills really creates a toasty texture.

Cooking Time: 10 minutes
Servings: 4
Ingredients:
- 8 slices of rye bread
- ½ cup thousand island dressing
- 1 ¼ cup sauerkraut
- 8 slices Swiss cheese
- 8 sliced corned beef
- 5 tbsp. butter

Directions:
1. Lightly butter the outside of all 8 slices of bread.
2. Cover each slice of rye bread with some dressing.
3. Divide the corned beef, cheese and sauerkraut onto 4 of the slices.
4. Cover with the remaining 4 slices.
5. Using medium heat, grill each sandwich by placing it in a skillet butter-side down.
6. Press the sandwich down by placing something heavy, such as a cast iron skillet, on top.
7. Grill for 5 minutes, flip the sandwich, press down the other side and grill for another 5 minutes.

Grilled Spicy Turkey and Bacon Sandwich

This wonderful sandwich gets a kick from the chipotle pepper. The recipe calls for a panini maker, but if you don't have one, use a grill or brown in a skillet.

Cooking Time: 27 minutes
Servings: 4
Ingredients:
- 8 bacon slices
- 2 minced garlic cloves
- 1 small sliced onion
- 3 cups fresh spinach leaves
- 1/3 cup mayonnaise
- ½ chopped and seeded chipotle peppers
- 8 ciabatta breads
- 4 slices mozzarella cheese
- ½ lb. sliced turkey meat – deli turkey is fine

Directions:
1. Fry the bacon in a skillet for about 10 minutes, until done.
2. Place the bacon on a paper towel and discard all but a tbsp. of bacon grease.
3. Sauté the onion and garlic in the bacon grease for 7-8 minutes.
4. Add the spinach and stir for 4 minutes.
5. Combine the mayonnaise and chopped pepper in a bowl.
6. Slice the ciabatta bread in half and top 4 slices with the mayonnaise mix.
7. Top the same 4 slices with turkey meat, cheese and 2 slices of bacon.
8. Add the onion/garlic/spinach mixture to the slices.
9. Top with the remaining slices of bread to create sandwiches.
10. Heat the panini maker and grill each sandwich for 5 minutes.

Thanksgiving Leftovers Sandwich

It's no big secret that many people want the Thanksgiving leftovers more than the actual turkey dinner. Some even roast a second turkey just to get leftovers! This sandwich is such a tasty treat. If you feel like going a bit crazy, add a tbsp. of mashed potatoes to each sandwich.

Cooking Time: 10 minutes
Servings: 2
Ingredients:
- 4 slices sourdough bread or 2 French baguettes
- 2 tbsp. mayonnaise
- 2 slices Swiss or cheddar cheese
- 6 oz. thinly sliced roasted turkey
- 4 tbsp. cranberry sauce, preferably homemade
- ¼ cup turkey dressing
- 2 tbsp. turkey gravy
- 3 tbsp. butter

Directions:
1. Spread the mayonnaise on 2 bread slices or 1 baguette slice.
2. Top with turkey and 1 slice of cheese.
3. Add the cranberry sauce and dressing.
4. Drizzle the dressing with gravy.
5. Top the sandwich or baguette to create a sandwich.
6. Melt the butter in a skillet.
7. Brown each sandwich for 4-5 minutes per side.

Mediterranean Sandwiches
Tuna Salad in Pita Pockets

A tuna salad with a Greek flavor. Make the salad the day before and refrigerate to allow the flavors to meld.

Cooking Time: 0
Servings: 2
Ingredients:
- 2 cans drained albacore tuna
- ¼ cup chopped Kalamata olives
- ¼ cup chopped celery stalks
- 1 diced red onion
- 1/3 cup sliced cucumbers
- Salt and pepper to taste
- 1 sliced tomatoes
- 2 slightly toasted pita pockets

Ingredients for Dressing:
- 3 tbsp. mayonnaise
- 1 tbsp. Dijon mustard
- 2 tbsp. lime juice
- 1 minced garlic clove

Directions:
1. Drain and crumble the tuna in a bowl.
2. Combine with the remaining Ingredients except for the tomatoes and pita.
3. Prepare the dressing by stirring together dressing Ingredients.
4. Toss the tuna salad with the dressing.
5. Stuff both pita pockets with the tuna salad and add tomato slices

Grilled Vegetable Sandwich

Grilled vegetable with goat cheese. A terrific way to use up vegetables.
Cooking Time: 20 minutes
Servings: 2
Ingredients:
- 2 tbsp. olive oil
- 3 minced garlic cloves
- 1 eggplant, sliced into strips
- 1 bell peppers cut into strips
- ½ cup chopped sun-dried tomatoes
- 2 sliced Portobello mushrooms
- ½ tsp. basil
- ½ tsp. thyme
- 4 oz. goat cheese
- 2 baguettes

Directions:
1. Heat the olive oil in a large skillet and sauté the garlic for 2 minutes
2. Add the eggplant, bell pepper sun-dried tomatoes and mushrooms.
3. Season with the herbs and let cook for about 5 minutes, until the vegetables have softened.
4. While the vegetables cook, slice the baguettes and add the goat cheese to each.
5. Stack the cooked vegetables onto the baguettes.
6. Place the sandwiches on a roasting sheet.
7. Roast the sandwiches for 10 – 12 minutes at 350 degrees.

Greek-Style Chicken Salad Sandwich

A refreshing chicken salad with not mayonnaise – just tasty vegetables and herbs.
Cooking Time: 5 minutes
Servings: 6
Ingredients:
- 1 ½ lb. chopped chicken meat (or get a rotisserie chicken)
- 1 tbsp. olive oil
- 2 diced tomatoes
- 1 chopped cucumber
- 1 small chopped onion
- 2 tbsp. balsamic vinegar
- 2 tbsp. olive oil
- 1 tsp. thyme
- ½ tsp. mint
- Salt and pepper to taste
- 4 tbsp. crumbled feta cheese
- 6 pita pockets, slightly toasted.

Directions:
1. Heat the oil in a skillet and brown the chicken pieces for 5 minutes. (If using a rotisserie chicken, skip this step. Just shred the meat.)
2. Place the chicken in a bowl and add the cucumbers, tomatoes and onions.
3. Whisk together the balsamic vinegar, olive oil and herbs.
4. Coat the chicken and vegetables with the dressing.
5. Refrigerate the salad for an hour.
6. Fill the pita pockets with the chicken salad and sprinkle with feta cheese.

Falafel and Cucumber Sauce

Falafels are a basic street food in Greece. They taste great fried, but if you want to make them healthier, you can bake them, as well.

Cooking Time: 6 minutes
Servings: 2

Ingredients for Sauce:
- 6 oz. plain Greek yogurt
- ½ cup chopped cucumber drained of liquid
- 1 tbsp. chopped parsley
- 1 tsp. dill
- 1 tsp. lemon juice
- Salt and pepper to taste

Ingredients for Falafel
- 15 oz. chickpeas, drained of liquid
- 1/3 cup chopped parsley
- 1 chopped onion
- 2 chopped garlic cloves
- 1 beaten egg
- 1 tsp. cumin
- Salt and pepper to taste
- 1/8 tsp red chili flakes
- 1 tsp. lemon juice
- 1 tbsp. flour
- 1 tbsp. olive oil
- 1 cup breadcrumbs
- ¼ cup canola oil
- 2 pita breads

Directions:
1. Mix together the sauce Ingredients and refrigerate for an hour.
2. Use a fork to smash the chickpeas.
3. Place the parsley, onion, and garlic in a blender and process to a paste
4. Combine the chickpeas and the onion paste.
5. Stir together the egg, spices, lemon juice and flour.
6. Add the mixture to the chickpeas and stir in the olive oil until combined.
7. Combine the mixture with the breadcrumbs
8. Create 8 patties.
9. Heat the canola oil in a skillet.
10. Fry the chickpea patties 3 minutes on each side.
11. Drain on a paper towel.
12. Fill each pita bread with 4 patties.
13. If desired, add chopped tomatoes and lettuce.
14. Serve with yogurt sauce.

Chicken Souvlaki

The marinade adds some real zest to this chicken. Serve with pita bread and the deliciously creamy sauce. A real treat.
Cooking Time: 10 minutes
Servings: 4
Souvlaki Ingredients:
- 4 chicken breasts
- 4 pita pockets
- 1 sliced onion
- 1 sliced tomato
- ¾ cup crumbled feta cheese

Marinade Ingredients:
- 4 tbsp. olive oil
- 1 tbsp. Greek seasoning
- 1 tbsp. diced garlic
- 3 tbs. tablespoons lemon juice
- 1 tbsp. oregano
- Salt and pepper to taste

Tzatziki Sauce Ingredients:
- 1 cup plain Greek yogurt
- ¾ cup shredded cucumber
- Salt and pepper to taste
- 2 minced garlic cloves
- 1 tbsp. white vinegar
- 1 tsp. olive oil
- 1 tbsp. chopped dill

Directions:
1. Mix together the marinade Ingredients and add the chicken in a plastic bag.
2. Shake well to coat and refrigerate for 2-3 hours.
3. Heat your outdoor grill for high heat.
4. Drain any excess liquid from the cucumbers by squeezing them.
5. Combine the Tzatziki sauce Ingredients, including the cucumber.
6. Place the chicken on the heated grill and cook for 10 minutes.
7. Cut the chicken into thin slices.
8. Lightly toast the pita pockets.
9. Divide the chicken, onions, tomatoes and feta cheese in the pita and add the Tzatziki sauce.

Hummus, Avocado Sandwich with Feta

This sandwich is perfect for lunch or dinner. There's no meat, but an abundance of flavors.

Cooking Time: 4 minutes
Servings: 2
Ingredients:
- 4 slices wheat or white bread
- 1/2 cup hummus
- ½ cup chopped roasted red pepper
- 2 avocados
- 1/4 cup crumbled feta cheese
- 1 sliced tomato
- 1 sliced onion
- ¼ cup baby spinach
- Salt and black pepper, to taste
- 2 tbsp. olive oil

Directions:
1. Spread 2 bread slices with the hummus.
2. Mash the avocado and feta cheese in a bowl.
3. Season with salt and pepper.
4. Spread the avocado on top of the hummus.
5. Top with tomato slices, onion slices, baby spinach and roasted red peppers.
6. Top the slices with the remaining 2 slices to create a sandwich.
7. Heat the olive oil in a skillet.
8. Grill the sandwiches 2 minutes on each side.

Hummus and Caramelized Onion Sandwich

This is a deceptively simple sandwich, but the tangy hummus and sweet caramelized onions work great together.

Cooking Time: 24 minutes
Servings: 2
Ingredients:
- 1 sliced onion
- 1 tbsp. olive oil
- ½ cup sliced mushrooms
- 8 tbsp. hummus
- Salt and pepper to taste
- 4 slices white bread

Directions:
1. Heat the olive oil in a skillet.
2. Brown the onions for 10 minutes.
3. Stir in the mushrooms and cook for another 7-8 minutes. The onions should be caramelized.
4. Grease a griddle.
5. Spread 2 sliced of bread with hummus.
6. Top both with the mushroom/onion mixture.
7. Season with salt and pepper.
8. Cover both slices with the remaining bread and cook for 3 minutes.
9. Flip the sandwich and cook for another 3 minutes.

Sandwiches from Around the World

Croque Monsieur

This delectable sandwich is a bit messy to eat, so it's best to use a knife and fork. Especially if you add the fried egg and turn it into a Croque Madame.

Cooking Time: 18 minutes
Servings: 4
Ingredients:
- ½ cup butter
- 3 tbsp. white flour
- 1/3 cup grated Parmesan cheese
- ¾ cup grated Gruyere cheese
- 8 sliced Gruyere cheese
- 8 sliced sourdough or country-style bread
- 12 ham slices, preferably French Jambon
- 2 tbsp. Dijon mustard

Directions:
1. Melt 4 tbsp. butter in a small pan and use a whisk to add the flour.
2. Stir in the milk and let the liquid simmer.
3. Keep stirring for about 5 minutes. This is a Bechamel sauce that should thicken.
4. Take the pan off the stove and stir in the grated Parmesan.
5. Use the remaining butter to spread over the bread slices
6. Place 4 bread slices on a baking sheet – buttered side down
7. To each of the 4 bread slices, add 2 Gruyere slices and slices of ham.
8. Spread the mustard on the remaining bread slices
9. Create four sandwiches.
10. Preheat the broiler.
11. Fry each sandwich in a skillet for 10 minutes, browning both sides.
12. Place the sandwiches on a baking sheet and top with the Bechamel sauce.
13. Broil for 3 minutes.
14. If you are preparing a Croque Madame, top each sandwich with a friend egg.

Paneer Sandwich

A creamy toasted cottage cheese sandwich from India that's infused with some savory spices.

Cooking Time: 15 minutes
Servings: 4
Ingredients:
- 1 ½ cup small-cured cottage cheese
- 2 tbsp. butter
- 1 diced onion
- 1 chopped red chili
- 1 tsp cumin seeds
- ¼ tsp. garam masala
- ¼ tsp. chili powder
- ½ tsp. turmeric powder
- 2 diced tomatoes
- ¼ tsp. turmeric powder
- Salt to taste
- 8 sandwich slices
- ¼ cup chopped coriander

Directions:
1. Melt the butter in a skillet.
2. Sauté the onion, chili and cumin seeds for 6-7 minutes.
3. Stir in the remaining spices and cook for 1 minute.
4. Add the diced tomatoes and stir well.
5. Season with salt.
6. Stir in the cottage cheese keep stirring for 4 minutes.
7. Turn off the stove.
8. Lay out four slices of bread.
9. Divide the paneer mixture between the four slices
10. Sprinkle each slice with the chopped coriander.
11. Top with remaining four slices to create sandwiches.
12. Place in a toaster oven or regular oven.
13. Toast the sandwiches until golden brown – 4 minutes each side.

Vietnamese Banh Mi

Banh Mi, a Vietnamese favorite, has lots of Ingredients. The flavors meld well together. The marinated vegetables are an important part of this sandwich, so prepare them ahead of time.

Cooking Time: 10 minutes
Servings: 4
Ingredients:
- 2 cups marinated shredded carrots and daikon radish (see recipe below)
- 2 tbsp. vegetable oil
- 4 pork chops
- Salt and pepper to taste
- ½ tsp. garlic salt
- 4 sliced French baguettes
- 3 tsp. mayonnaise
- ¼ cup lime juice
- 1 oz. chili sauce
- 1 sliced red onion
- 2 chopped jalapeno peppers
- 1 sliced cucumber
- 2 tbsp. chopped chives
- 2 tablespoons chopped fresh cilantro
- Salt and pepper to taste
- ¼ tsp. Maggi seasoning

Directions:
1. Season the pork chops with salt, pepper and garlic salt.
2. Heat the vegetable oil in a skillet and brown the chops for 5 minutes each side.
3. Lightly toast the baguettes in the oven for 5 minutes.
4. Slit the baguettes and spread with some mayonnaise.
5. Top each baguette with a pork chop and drizzle with lime juice.
6. Add chili sauce, onion slices jalapeno pepper, cucumber slices, chives and cilantro to each baguette.
7. Season with salt and pepper and sprinkle with Maggi
8. Top with the marinated shredded carrots and daikon radish.

Pickled Carrot and Daikon Radish
Ingredients:
- 1 cup julienned carrots
- 1 cup julienned daikon radish
- 4 tbsp. white sugar
- 2 tbsp. salt
- ½ cup white vinegar

Directions:
1. Mix the vinegar, sugar and salt with 2 cups of water and stir.
2. Add the julienned vegetables
3. Transfer into sealable plastic container and marinate in refrigerator for up to 3 days

Thai Peanut Chicken Sandwich

An unusually savory and spicy sauce made with peanut butter. Simply delicious.
Cooking Time: 18 minutes
Servings: 6
Ingredients:
- 6 skinless and boneless chicken breasts
- 12 fried and drained bacon slices
- 6 brioches

Ingredients for Marinade:
- ¼ cup peanut oil
- 4 tbsp. soy sauce
- 1 tsp. grated ginger
- ½ tbsp. onion powder
- ½ tbsp. garlic powder
- ½ tbsp. paprika
- Salt and pepper to taste
- 1 tbsp. red pepper flakes
- Dash of cayenne pepper

Ingredients for Peanut Sauce
- ½ cup coconut milk
- 1 cup crunchy peanut butter
- 2 tbsp. soy sauce
- 1 diced jalapeno pepper
- 3 tbsp. white wine vinegar
- 1 tbsp. peanut oil

Directions:
1. Mix together the marinade in a bowl and coat the chicken with the marinade
2. Cover the bowl and refrigerate for up to 12 hours.
3. Grill the chicken until it is done – 10-15 minutes.
4. Place all sauce Ingredients in a pan and heat to a simmer.
5. Stir and cook for 3 minutes.
6. Let the sauce cool.
7. Cut open the brioches and add the chicken breasts and bacon.
8. Drizzle the sauce over the sandwich and use remaining sauce for dipping.

Thai Beef Lettuce Wraps

These crunchy/sweet wraps are perfect to pack for lunch. Sure, beats those boring sandwiches everyone else at the office is having.

Cooking Time:
Servings: 2
Ingredients:
- 1/3 cup bean sprouts
- ½ cup shredded carrots
- 1/2 cup fresh mint leaves
- 2 tbsp. Thai chili sauce
- 2 teaspoons lime juice
- 2 tsp. brown sugar
- 2 flour tortilla wraps
- 4 Bibb lettuce leaves
- ½ peeled and sliced cucumber
- 4 slices rare roast beef
- ½ sliced onion
- Salt and pepper to taste

Directions:
1. Combine the bean sprouts, shredded carrots and mint leaves in a bowl.
2. In another bowl, stir together the chili sauce, brown sugar and lime juice.
3. Place the tortilla wraps on a surface and top each with a Bibb lettuce.
4. Top the wraps with roast beef, sliced cucumbers, onion sliced and bean sprout mixture
5. Drizzle each wrap with the sauce mixture.
6. Roll up the tortilla wraps.

Cuban Sandwich

The Cuban sandwich is fun, and it always reminds of us someone trying to decide what to put on a sandwich and then using everything. It's great tasting, though, and the pickles are a must. They add just the right amount of pizzazz.

Cooking Time: 16 minutes
Servings: 8
Ingredients:
- 8 slices Cuban bread
- ¼ cup mayonnaise
- 2 tbsp. spicy mustard
- ½ lb. cooked and sliced roast pork
- 1/2 pound cooked ham (thinly sliced)
- ½ lb. salami
- ¾ cup dill pickle slices
- 1/2 pound thinly sliced Swiss cheese
- 3 tbsp. olive oil
- 3 tbsp. softened butter

Directions:
1. Stir the mayonnaise and the mustard together
2. Spread the mixture on 4 Cuban bread slices.
3. Top each slice with slices of roast pork, ham, salami and cheese.
4. Add pickle slices to each.
5. Top with the remaining slices of Cuban bread to create a sandwich.
6. Brush the top of each sandwich with olive oil and the bottom with butter.
7. Heat a skillet and cook each sandwich for 2 minutes on each side. Use a griddle press to flatten the sandwich.

Cucumber Tea Sandwiches

If it's good enough for the queen, wouldn't you want to try one? Cucumber sandwiches are light and delicious. They aren't really a lunch-type sandwich. Tea sandwiches were created when a hungry English duchess tried to survive the long hours between lunch and a late dinner. Her cook created a few delicacies and saved the day by serving them around four o'clock. Host your own tea, or serve these on a tray before dinner while guests are still mingling. Hint: a great way to get paper-thin cucumber slices is to use a cheese cutter.

Cooking Time: 0
Servings: 16 or 32
Ingredients:
- 1 large cucumber, peeled and thinly sliced
- 8 oz. cream cheese
- ¼ cup mayonnaise
- ¼ tsp. garlic powder
- ½ tsp Worcestershire sauce
- Dash of pepper
- 16 slices thin white bread
- 2 tsp. dill

Directions:
1. Slice the cucumber into very thin slices.
2. Place them in a bowl with a dash of salt and refrigerate for 1-2 hours. This will remove the excess liquid.
3. Whisk the mayonnaise, cream cheese, garlic powder, Worcestershire sauce and pepper by hand or in a blender.
4. Remove the crust from the bread.
5. Spread half the bread slices with the mayonnaise/cream cheese.
6. Add the cucumber slices and top with a dash of dill.
7. Top with the remaining bread slices.
8. Cut each sandwich into half or quarters.

English Sausage Rolls

Sausage rolls are a bit heartier than the cucumber sandwiches and 2 make a great lunch.

Cooking Time: 28 minutes
Servings: 12
Ingredients:
- 1 lb. pork sausage
- 1 small diced onion
- 1 tbsp. olive oil
- ½ tsp. onion powder
- ½ tsp. sage
- Salt and pepper to taste
- 1 thawed package of frozen puff pastry
- ¼ cup Dijon mustard
- 3 beaten eggs

Directions:
1. Preheat the oven to 400 degrees.
2. Heat the olive oil in a skillet and sauté the onions for 5 minutes.
3. Stir in the crumbled pork sausage and fry for around 3 minutes, just enough to get rid of some of the fat. Drain the fat. Set aside.
4. Cut the puff pastry in 12 squares.
5. Top each of the squares with the Dijon mustard.
6. Add 2 beaten eggs and the seasoning to the sausage meat.
7. Divide the meat into each pastry square.
8. Roll the pastry squares into logs.
9. Place the logs on a baking sheet and brush with remaining beaten egg.
10. Bake for 20 minutes.

Herring and Onion on Pumpernickel

In Scandinavia, they savor a good herring. It's a fatty, rich fish that's a genuine indulgence. A good pumpernickel or rye brings out the fish's best flavors.

Cooking Time: 0
Servings: 8
Ingredients:
- 3 tbsp. softened butter
- 4 pumpernickel or rye bread slices
- 8 oz. herring fillets (in wine sauce) cut into thin strips.
- 1 sliced red onion
- 1 thinly sliced tomato
- 1 tsp. lemon juice
- 2 tbsp. capers
- Garnish with parsley

Directions:
1. Lay out the bread slices and top them generously with butter.
2. Cut the bread slices in half.
3. Top each slice with a tomato slice, onion slice and herring.
4. Drizzle with lemon juice and sprinkle with the capers.
5. Garnish with chopped parsley.

Chicken Parmesan Sandwich

This chicken parmesan is kicked up several notches by brining the chicken first. If you are new to brining, you will be shocked at the difference it makes. Brined chicken is so unbelievably juicy, you'll never eat chicken any other way.

Cooking Time: 13 minutes
Servings: 4
Ingredients:

- 4 boneless, skinless chicken breasts.
- 6 tbsp. salt
- ½ cup white flour
- 4 tbsp. parmesan cheese
- ¾ cup bread crumbs
- 1 beaten egg
- Salt and pepper to taste
- ½ tsp. oregano
- ½ tsp. basil
- ½ tsp. garlic salt
- 2 tbsp. olive oil
- 1 cup tomato sauce, preferably homemade
- ½ cup shredded mozzarella
- 4 hoagie rolls

Directions:
1. Place the chicken in a bowl.
2. Cover with water and stir in the salt.
3. Refrigerate for up to 12 hours.
4. Remove the chicken from the water and let dry. It's important that the chicken is dried before frying.
5. In a shallow dish, combine the flour with the oregano, basil, garlic salt, pepper and salt.
6. In another dish, mix the bread crumbs with the parmesan cheese.
7. Place the beaten egg in a third dish.
8. Use a mallet to pound the chicken until it is thin.
9. Dredge the chicken pieces through the seasoned flour, then the egg, and lastly the bread crumb mixture.
10. Heat the olive oil in a large skillet and fry the chicken 5 minutes each side.
11. Drain the chicken on a paper towel.
12. Place the 4 hoagie rolls on a baking sheet.
13. Fill the rolls with 1 chicken piece each, then top with the tomato sauce and shredded mozzarella cheese.
14. Place under the broiler for 3 minutes, until the cheese is bubbly.

Meatball Submarine

The meatballs and sauce can be prepared ahead of time. While you can use a jarred sauce, the meatball sub tastes infinitely better with a homemade sauce.

Cooking Time: 1 hour 7 minutes
Servings: 4
Ingredients:

- ½ lb. ground beef
- ½ lb. ground pork
- 2/3 cup bread crumbs
- ½ tsp. oregano
- ½ tsp. garlic salt
- ½ tsp. thyme
- ½ tsp. basil
- ½ tsp. red pepper flakes
- 2 minced garlic cloves
- 3 tbsp. chopped parsley
- 3 tbsp. Parmesan cheese
- 1 beaten egg
- 1 tbsp. olive oil.
- 1 long French baguette or 4 hoagie rolls
- 2 cups tomato sauce, preferably homemade
- 4 slices provolone cheese

Directions:
1. Preheat the oven to 350 degrees.
2. Mix the beef, pork, bread crumbs, seasonings, parsley, garlic, beaten egg and Parmesan cheese in a bowl.
3. Create 12 meatballs.
4. Heat the olive oil and brown the meatballs for 5 minutes.
5. Place the meatballs in a large pot and top with the tomato sauce.
6. Simmer for 50 minutes to an hour.
7. Heat the oven to 350 degrees and toast the baguette or hoagies for 7 minutes
8. Remove the bread, but keep the oven on.
9. Use a tong to transfer the meatballs to the bread and spoon the sauce over the meatballs
10. Top the meatballs with mozzarella cheese.
11. Place the subs on a baking sheet and return to oven.
12. Cook until the cheese is melted, about 5 minutes.
13. If using a baguette, cut into 4 pieces.

Russian Kielbasa Sandwich

These sandwiches are eaten either at tea or at any other time. If you can find good, black Russian bread, use it. Otherwise, rye bread will be fine.

Cooking: 0
Servings: 2
Ingredients:
- 4 slices rye bread
- 2 tbsp. butter
- 2 slices Havarti cheese
- ½ cup sliced kielbasa
- ½ sliced small cucumber
- 1 tbsp. dill

Directions:
1. Spread the butter on two slices of bread.
2. Add the kielbasa slices and Havarti.
3. Top with cucumber slices and dill.
4. Create sandwiches with the remaining slices of bread.

Stromboli

How clever of the Italians to make a sandwich with pizza dough. This has lots of meats and vegetables. You can add or subtract your favorites. It's pretty much a make-your-own pizza sandwich.

Cooking Time: 30 minutes
Servings: 6
Ingredients:
- 10 oz. pizza crust dough
- 1 lb. crumbled sausage meat
- ½ tsp. thyme
- ½ tsp. oregano
- ½ tsp. garlic salt
- ½ cup sliced ham
- ½ cup sliced Genoa salami
- 1 chopped bell pepper
- 1 chopped onion
- 1 ½ cup marinara sauce
- ½ cup canned mushrooms
- 4 tbsp. melted butter
- 1 cup sliced pepperoni
- 1 cup shredded mozzarella cheese

Directions:
1. Preheat the oven to 400 degrees.
2. Brown the sausage meat in a skillet for 5 minutes.
3. Stir in the thyme, oregano and garlic salt.
4. Add the ham, salami, onions, mushroom and peppers and stir.
5. Pour in the marinara sauce and combine well.
6. Place the pizza dough on a baking sheet.
7. Top the dough with the peperoni slices.
8. Place the meat/sauce mixture on half of the dough.
9. Top with the shredded mozzarella.
10. Flip the empty dough side over the filling and use your fingers to close the ends.
11. Cut a few slices in the dough and drizzle with melted butter.
12. Bake for 30 minutes.
13. Cut the Stromboli into pieces.

Bean Burritos

These are meatless burritos, but you can add meat, if you want. They are not too spicy, so if you crave heat, add a dash of hot sauce.

Cooking Time: 15 minutes
Servings: 2
Ingredients:
- 2 flour tortillas
- ¾ cup refried beans
- ½ tsp. garlic powder
- 1 tbsp. olive oil
- ½ diced onion
- ½ cup diced bell peppers
- ½ cup grated cheddar cheese
- ¼ cup tomato salsa
- Salt and pepper to taste
- 4 tbsp. sour cream
- 1 tbsp. olive oil

Directions:
1. Heat the refried beans in a pan and stir in the garlic powder.
2. Heat the olive oil in a skillet and sauté the onions and peppers for 5 minutes.
3. Clean the skillet or use another to warm the tortillas for 2-3 minutes each side
4. With the tortillas on a flat surface, add the shredded cheddar, peppers, onions, tomatoes, sour cream, salsa, salt and pepper.
5. Roll up the tortillas and secure the ends.
6. Heat the remaining olive oil in a skillet and warm the burritos for 7-8 minutes.

Steak Torta

A Mexican grilled steak filled with refried beans and avocados. Seriously delicious.
Cooking Time: 12 minutes
Servings: 4
Ingredients:
- 1 lb. sirloin steak
- ½ tbsp. garlic salt
- ½ tsp. pepper
- Dash of cayenne pepper
- ½ tsp. garlic powder
- 4 torta rolls or kaiser rolls
- 1/3 cup mayonnaise
- 1 tbsp. chopped chipotle in adobe sauce
- 1/2 cup refried beans
- 1 sliced avocado
- 1 sliced tomato
- ½ cup sliced chorizo
- ½ cup shredded Monterey Pepper Jack cheese

Directions:
1. Preheat the grill.
2. Season the sirloin with the spices and pepper.
3. Grill the steak to medium-rare and cover with aluminum foil.
4. Combine the mayonnaise and chipotle in adobe sauce
5. Spread the mayonnaise on two split rolls.
6. Brown the rolls for 3-4 minutes.
7. Heat the refried beans in a pan or in the microwave.
8. When steak is done, slice into thin strips.
9. Spoon the refried bean on half of the split rolls and top with steak slices, chorizo slices, avocado and tomato.
10. Sprinkle with shredded cheese.

www.ingramcontent.com/pod-product-compliance
Lightning Source LLC
Chambersburg PA
CBHW081128080526
44587CB00021B/3785